Esther was a beautiful Jewish girl living in the land of Persia.

She was an orphan brought up by her good cousin Mordecai.

The King decided to choose a new Queen. Esther and many other girls were presented to the King.

King Ahasuerus chose Esther to be the new queen.

Proud Haman the king's servant hated Mordecai.

He passed a law plotting to kill all the Jews. He built some gallows to kill Mordecai on.

Mordecai mourned deeply about this sad news.

He told Esther the problem. "Can you do anything? Who knows but you may have been made queen for this time."

Esther went to see the king.

She invited
the king and Haman
to a big feast.

"Do not kill me and my people" she begged.

The king was angry
with Haman.

Haman was punished
on the gallows he had built
for Mordecai.

News was sent round the land ~the Jews were not to be killed.

Mordecai was honoured by the king.

The Jewish people had a big party to celebrate.